Protecting the Vatican

The Mysterious History of the Swiss Guard

Conrad Bauer

ISBN: 9781701377400

Printed in the United States

MAPLEWOOD
PUBLISHING

Contents

The Swiss Guard through the Ages   *1*

The Hit Men of the Guard—Operation Pigeon Revealed   *3*

The Day John Paul II Let his Guard Down   *9*

Guarding Against the Vatican Bank Scandal   *17*

Alois Estermann and the Swiss Swirl of Conspiracy   *25*

Guarding the World's Largest Closet   *31*

The Bliss of Being Swiss   *35*

Further Readings   *37*

The Swiss Guard through the Ages

On the 6th of May in the year 1527, a group of some 42 members of the Swiss Guard were vigorously providing the security detail for a pope who was fleeing for his life.

The pope we speak of was Pope Clement VII, and due to the growing political tensions of his day he was a pope whose grip on temporal power had been weakening rapidly. Now, a sudden role reversal in European power politics was threatening to end his reign outright. The man who was supposed to be the pope's defender, Holy Roman Emperor Charles V, had decided that he knew how to run the Catholic Church better than the Holy Father, and he was ready to wage war in order to prove his supremacy. In the heated cauldron that was brewing, Clement found himself at increasing risk of being forcibly seized and arrested.

So it was that on the morning of May 6, 1527, the Swiss Guard quickly hustled the pope out through a secret corridor away from St. Peter's Basilica and on down to a fortress that was specially built for just such a siege—Castel Sant'Angelo. Their bold and decisive escort allowed the pope to escape certain arrest and most likely certain death—death that the pope, now secure in his fortress, could see and hear all around him as the forces of the Holy Roman Emperor laid waste to the papal estates. The carnage that ensued was absolutely horrific, and wearing priestly vestments was no safeguard against being slaughtered.

The pope's successful escape from Charles' clutches was a stunning achievement, but it came at a great cost. The 42 guardsmen who accompanied the pope were only those who had managed to survive the opening rounds of the conflict. Another 147 members of the Guard had given their lives to ensure that the Pope's rescue could occur.

Fighting like ferocious lions, these guardsmen threw themselves forward as the main imperial army approached the gates of the basilica. Swinging their halberds and long swords in a frenzy, they inflicted far more casualties than they took—but even the phenomenal fighting ability of the Swiss Guard, who numbered less than 200 that day, would not be able to withstand the thousands of troops arrayed against them. Fortunately, for the purpose of protecting the pope that day, they didn't have to. They merely needed to hold off the enemy long enough for a smaller contingent of guardsmen to escort the pope to safety. And this feat they achieved with flying colors.

The Swiss Guard had proven themselves to be more-than-capable fighters who were willing to put their lives on the line for the papacy, and it was because of bold and tenacious efforts such as this that the pope made them a permanent institution. 500 years later, Pope Francis is still guarded by several colorfully clad Swiss with long halberds straight out of the Middle Ages.

Of course, the uniforms and medieval weaponry are mostly just for show. But there's nothing ceremonial about the Guard's sacred role as protector of the faith. Because along with those halberds, the guardsmen have fully automatic firearms and extensive training in marital arts. If push came to shove, they would be still be more than ready to put up a fight. Even now, the Swiss Guard is tracking many modern threats that the papacy may face. If the likes of ISIS, for example, dared to launch an assault on the Vatican, you'd better believe that the fierce wielders of the halberd have a contingency plan in place!

But as honorable as the history of the Swiss Guard has been in many respects, over the centuries they have courted more than their fair share of intrigue and controversy. This book takes a look at some of the more mysterious history surrounding the Swiss Guard and the organizations associated with it. Here you will find of tales of intrigue, mystery, heroic exploits and then some. If you thought you knew your history when it came to the Swiss Guard—think again.

The Hit Men of the Guard— Operation Pigeon Revealed

The Swiss Guard certainly have much to be proud of in their storied, steadfast history of protecting the pope through the centuries. They have undoubtedly foiled numerous plots against his life. But has this always been the case? If you believe some insiders at the Vatican, there may have been times that the Guard somehow... well, let their guard down. And some would even go so far as to suggest that there have been times when the Swiss Guard, rather than protecting the pope, has actively targeted him!

This is part of the premise of the so-called Operation Pigeon, in which it is alleged that a mysterious cabal including the Swiss Guard was responsible for the sudden death of Pope John Paul I, the immediate predecessor of John Paul II. The mystery began when the pope was found dead in his bed with a newspaper in his hand. It was a strange sight to say the least. There was the pope, perfectly undisturbed, as if he were about to turn the next page of the paper—yet he was dead as a doornail. The position of the pope with the newspaper in his hand was so chillingly perfect it almost seemed like it was staged. In fact, many forensics experts would later insist that it *was* staged. They believe that the pope was murdered and his body positioned in this macabre display by his wily killers.

So, what did officials at the Vatican have to say about the odd state of the pope's mortal remains? Their only response was that his death occurred "by the grace of God." According to them, the pope suffered an abrupt cardiovascular event. Whether it was a stroke or a heart attack is not exactly clear, but apparently it happened while he was in the middle of reading his newspaper.

Of course, the Vatican's declaration that Pope John Paul I died through divine providence, together with the vagueness of the official ruling as to the cause, served to fuel a certain amount of skepticism over what may have actually happened. So let's play along. Say that the pope did indeed fall victim to foul play—what would be the reason for it? Well, given the pope's position as head of the Catholic Church and sovereign of Vatican City, the most obvious reason would be the papal succession. Who would be the next pope?

We know, of course, that the baton was eventually passed to the Polish Cardinal Karol Józef Wojtyła, who took on the name of his predecessor and became Pope John Paul II. But the name was about where the similarities between the two popes ended. During his extremely short tenure (just 33 days!), John Paul I was widely viewed as a "moderate who had an open mind to changing canon." He was, for example, the first pope to rule that babies created through the process of artificial insemination had souls. This may seem uncontroversial to us now, but there had been long-winded debates in the halls of the Vatican over the issue of "ensoulment", and many cardinals felt that test tube babies just didn't make the cut. It's a little-known fact that as soon as John Paul II came to power, he reversed the determination John Paul I had made just a few weeks before. The Vatican's internal debate over whether children conceived by artificial insemination have souls would then continue for some time.

But this was not the only thing that was being debated. The Vatican bigwigs were also rather fond of arguing over the Church's role in fighting communism. On this issue, John Paul II had gained more than a few fans in America's CIA back when he was still Cardinal Wojtyła. A fan base in the CIA? Well, this wasn't exactly the Mickey Mouse Club; the reason the CIA took a deep interest in the Polish Cardinal was because of his overt, hardline stance against communism. Poland was on the other side of the Iron Curtain in those days, and to have a religious figure as high ranking as Cardinal Karol Wojtyła denouncing communism from within a communist country was highly pleasing to the American intelligence community. John Paul I, the moderate son of a socialist? Not so much.

So, from a strategic standpoint, the CIA had its reasons for wanting to replace John Paul I with John Paul II. But what about the Swiss Guard? How do they fit into this conspiracy/cover up (if there is one)? Well, just minutes after the pope was found dead on that fateful morning, Sergeant Hans Roggen, the head of the Swiss Guard, was in the courtyard of the Vatican Bank speaking with Archbishop Paul Marcinkus, the president of said bank. And why was it so essential to speak to the man who ran the bank at this moment? It all goes back to the pope's reading material at the time of his demise. While he was reportedly reading a newspaper, it turns out that what the dead pontiff held in his hands wasn't *L'Osservatore Romano* but rather a set of official documents from the Vatican Bank!

Strangely enough—or maybe not so strangely if you're willing to believe in a conspiracy theory or two—the pope was clutching important paperwork regarding a monumental decision he was about to make that would fundamentally alter the operation of the Vatican Bank. He and Marcinkus had apparently had a major falling out over how the bank should be run. In particular, John Paul I disapproved of Marcinkus allowing the bank to be taken over by Roberto Calvi's infamous Banco Ambrosiano. A whole book could be written on the sordid Ambrosiano affair (and we will revisit it in the following chapters), but the important point for now is that conspiracy theorists allege that the pope was just "a day away" from removing Marcinkus as president of the Vatican Bank. And guess who the official Swiss Guard report notes was found outside the papal apartments on that fateful morning? Why, none other than Paul Marcinkus! Coincidence? Conspiracy theorists think not!

So it would appear (to some) that we have a cabal of CIA agents and corrupt Vatican bankers suborning the Swiss Guard to take out the very man they were sworn to protect. Because if we are to believe in this conspiracy theory, it means that Roggen must have ordered his subordinates to turn a blind eye while unknown assailants entered the papal apartments. Swiss Guards were posted at every door of the compound, so unless there was a sudden Swiss Guard strike or really tasty donuts in the break room, the guards should have been there. So if we believe that the pope was indeed murdered, we have to believe that the Swiss Guard knew about it—and was in fact complicit in the crime.

These are the conspiratorial musings that have been alleged since that fateful day when the pope was found dead "by the grace of God". Can we believe them? God only knows.

The Day John Paul II Let his Guard Down

It had been a long day for the pope, and May 13, 1981, was turning into an even busier evening as Pope John Paul II left the safety of St. Peter's Basilica to greet pilgrims in St. Peter's Square. Although this was a routine, weekly event, due to this pope's rising popularity, one never knew quite what to expect. Pope John Paul II was loved for his unique personality and his compassion for the average person faced with forces beyond their control. And for those being oppressed by communist regimes during the Cold War, such as the people of his own native Poland, John Paul II was like a ray of light shining through the dark shadow cast by the Iron Curtain. So those who made the pilgrimage to Rome to see the pontiff were always lively and enthusiastic. The crowds were often more akin to what you might expect at a rock concert than a religious service.

This was the case on May 13, 1981, as the jubilant crowd cheered on the grinning John Paul II who came to greet them. It was nearly 5:00 PM when the pope arrived astride his "Popemobile"—a small white jeep from which he could wave at and address the pilgrims. About 20 minutes later, in the midst of continual cheers, camera flashes, and hand waving, four gunshots were heard and a wounded John Paul II staggered and fell into the Swiss Guardsmen who surrounded him as his papal vestments became soaked in blood.

The guardsmen sprang into action immediately. The gunman, Mehmet Ali Ağca, sprinted away through the crowd hoping to make a clean getaway in the ensuing panic, but a quick-thinking guardsman named Camillo Cibin grabbed him. Assisted by an angry nun, Cibin then detained Ağca until help arrived. Meanwhile, another guardsman by the name of Alois Estermann rushed over and shielded the pope with his own body. Estermann would later be promoted for his heroism and continue to rise through the ranks of the Swiss Guard until he was murdered in 1998; we will explore his death and the mystery surrounding him in a later chapter of this book.

As for the pope's injuries that day, those to his lower intestine were of the most concern. He had also received minor flesh wounds where a bullet struck his left index finger and one of his arms. Luckily, none of his vital organs were hit, but fearing internal bleeding from the wounds to his abdomen, the Swiss Guard quickly escorted him to the hospital—and escorted Ağca to jail. Found on his person was a note proclaiming his intent to assassinate the pope.

John Paul II recovered and lived for another 20 years, but he was meant to die that day, and someone wanted to make it clear who was responsible. As Ağca would obviously have been able to take responsibility if he was alive and talking, the note must have been for the event that he was killed or incapacitated during the assassination. But why was it so important to identify him as the pope's assassin? The answers to this question are not easy, especially since Ağca's own reasoning seems to have changed just about every other day.

On some occasions the attack was to fight what Ağca termed "imperialism", and on other occasions it was for religious reasons. At one point he blurted out that he had actually wanted to kill the King of England, but upon realizing that there was no King of England at the moment he had settled on the pope instead. And why not simply shift his sights to Queen Elizabeth II, if he had some beef with the British monarchy? Well, according to Ağca, as a Turkish Muslim, killing a woman would have been *haram*—a big no-no—for him. Indeed, a number of the answers that Ağca gave to his interrogators struck them as so absurd that they immediately suspected that he had been coached. It seemed like Ağca was attempting to keep them focused solely on him so they wouldn't seek any connections elsewhere.

But who or what was this would-be assassin attempting to cover for? Taking a look at Ağca's background we find a rather nebulous past. He was at one time part of a Turkish terrorist organization called the Grey Wolves. This ultra-nationalist group took its name from the Turkish legend of grey wolves leading the Turkish tribes from East Asia to settle on the Anatolian plains of Asia Minor (Turkey) thousands of years ago. It has been established that the Grey Wolves were—at least at one point—funding and orchestrating Ağca's movements, and they were behind literally hundreds of similar assassinations all over the world.

Ağca himself was already responsible for at least one other killing. In 1979 he had shot Turkish journalist Abdi İpekçi simply for opposing the extremism espoused by Ağca and his cohorts. He was convicted and sent to death row at a Turkish military prison, but he was somehow able to slip into a soldier's uniform and simply walk right out of the facility. Either Ağca was a criminal mastermind—which seemed a little unlikely considering his rambling responses to his interrogators—or he had had considerable help from the outside.

At any rate, Ağca spent the next two years on the run, traveling all around the Middle East, Eastern Europe and ultimately Italy while leaving a string of forged passports in his wake. It is unclear what much of this travel was about, although some have suggested that it was merely to create confusion as to his origins and shake potential investigators off of his trail.

At one point Ağca claimed that his attempt on the pope's life was directed by the Bulgarian intelligence service, which was in turn working for Russia's KGB. However, he quickly backpedaled on these claims, disavowing any larger conspiracy and professing that he acted alone, simply because God told him to. He turned his trial into a soap opera with outrageous statements such as the claim that he was an incarnation of Jesus who was heralding the imminent end of the age.

These may seem like the ramblings of a madman, but one of Ağca's rambles managed to hit upon a deep secret of the Vatican that by all accounts he should have known nothing about: Ağca revealed that he knew all about the "third secret of Fatima" which supposedly prophesied the assassination of the pope.

For those who aren't up on their Marian apparitions, the secrets of Fatima stemmed from visions witnessed by three peasant children in Fatima, Portugal, in 1917. In a series of fantastical experiences—the third of which was witnessed by hundreds of onlookers—the children were visited by a celestial being they perceived to be the Virgin Mary. The first vision seemed to revolve around the horrors of World War I and World War II. The second seemed to relate to the rise of communism. The third vision was the most shocking, since it seemed to show the assassination of a sitting pope. Most shocking of all, no one other than the children and a few Vatican higher-ups knew about this third and final secret of Fatima, because the Vatican had decided to lock it up so tight that even the Swiss Guard wouldn't be able to access it.

The secret would eventually be revealed to the world by John Paul II only a few years before his death. On May 13, 2000, the pope made a pilgrimage to Fatima even as Vatican Secretary of State Angelo Sodano finally released the contents of the third secret, announcing that it was a revelation that "a bishop clothed in white [will] fall to the ground, dead, under a burst of gunfire." John Paul II narrowly escaped this fate; whether the vision involves a future papal assassination remains to be seen. But the thing is, however you interpret the prophecy, prior to 2000, no one outside the tightest inner circle of the Vatican should have known anything about it. So how in the world did Ağca know the contents of this "secret" in the early 1980s?

Well, the secret was read by every single pope, of course, but there were also certain cardinals in the know as well. The future Pope Benedict XVI, previously known as Cardinal Joseph Ratzinger, was one of them. In 1996, when doomsday enthusiasts were clamoring all over creation that the year 2000 would end in Armageddon—and some among them were suggesting that the third secret must say as much—it was Ratzinger who stood up and declared that it would be a "perversion" to release the secret due to "public pressure." Ratzinger shrugged off the revelation by stating that "the Virgin [Mary] does not engage in sensationalism; she does not create fear."

At any rate, if Cardinal Ratzinger knew of the secret ahead of time, who else might have known? Could a cardinal such as Ratzinger have whispered the secret to one of the Swiss Guards? That is certainly possible; and then the question is—how would this information travel from the Swiss Guard to the ears of an eager assassin such as Ağca?

Well, that actually seems to be covered by the third secret of Fatima too. In 2004, Ratzinger alluded to aspects of the secret of the secret that were not divulged in the 2000 announcement, including a "wicked council" and a "bad Mass". This seems to indicate conspiratorial plotting within the walls of the Vatican itself, with clergy being part of the wicked council.

Could this wicked council have filled Ağca in on the third secret of Fatima? Could it even have hired him to commit what essentially amounted to an inside job on the Vatican's highest office? Did the Swiss Guard not only let their guard down but actively seek the demise of the man they were meant to protect? Were they part of the wicked council? This, of course, is all just speculation—but with enough intrigue to give *The Da Vinci Code* a run for its money, one can only wonder.

Guarding Against the Vatican Bank Scandal

The Vatican Bank—there is just about no other financial institution on the planet steeped in as much mystery and intrigue as this one repository of papal wealth. And one of the greatest of these intrigues involves the untimely death of a prestigious financial associate of the Vatican—known as God's Banker, in fact—by the name of Roberto Calvi. His passing was not an easy one; he was found hanged underneath a bridge in London with bricks stuffed in his pockets. Inevitably, from the grisly scene of Calvi's demise, conspiracy theories of a wide-ranging cabal involving the Mafia, the Vatican, and the Freemasons began to emerge.

In order to understand how this web was woven, first you need to know a little more about Calvi's background. He was the chairman of the second largest bank in Italy, the financial powerhouse called Banco Ambrosiano. Even before his infamous death, he was a well-known figure whom the papers often jokingly referred to as "God's Banker" in light of the intricate partnerships he had crafted with the Catholic Church. For quite some time, Roberto Calvi was the envy of Italy, with wealth, prestige and a good reputation to boot.

However, that reputation began to sour in 1978 (coincidentally or not the same year that Pope John Paul I died), and Banco Ambrosiano found itself being audited. Investigators discovered that billions of lire had somehow been funneled out of Italy and into various shell corporations overseas. This illegal migration of financial assets would turn into one of the most massive money laundering cases of all time. To make a long and sordid story short, Calvi was placed under arrest and charged with being the architect of the whole scheme.

Calvi always maintained his innocence, and as he was pressed by authorities, he would come to assert that he was just the fall guy, the stooge of a conspiratorial circle that few could have ever imagined. And the few who could imagine it apparently didn't include the prosecutors, because it was Calvi who stood trial, was convicted, and was handed a four-year sentence and a fine amounting to nearly 20 million U.S. dollars.

Calvi didn't serve his full term, but during his brief time as a prisoner he had a horrible go of it. Distressed and terribly depressed, Calvi was not able to adjust to prison life and reportedly sought to end it all by slashing his wrist and overdosing on pills. Upon being revived he simply stated that he had succumbed to a "fit of depression." Calvi got out on bail shortly thereafter, and incredibly enough, he returned to his role at the bank while his appeal was pending.

It was during the appeals process, in 1982, that Calvi fired off a strange missive to Pope John Paul II. He seemed to implicate the Vatican in the mess that he had been caught up in, and stated that if he didn't get papal cooperation on his case, "a catastrophe of unimaginable proportions in which the Church will suffer the gravest danger" would erupt.

The Vatican was indeed in an interesting place at the time of Calvi's appeal. Because it was the Vatican Bank which was the primary shareholder of Banco Ambrosiano, with its tentacles wrapped firmly around the failing financial institution. When, a short time after Calvi's ominous letter, Banco Ambrosiano finally went belly up, in the red by about 1.5 billion dollars, it was none other than the Vatican Bank that committed itself to paying 225 million dollars of what Ambrosiano owed. Why? That's the same question would-be prosecutors were asking themselves—purely as a theoretical exercise, however, because in the midst of the chaos, the Vatican had already asked for and received immunity from prosecution in the case!

Flash forward a few days, and Roberto Calvi was on a plane to London. Shortly afterward he was stripped of his title at the bank. An even more shocking development occurred almost simultaneously when Calvi's personal secretary, Graziella Corrocher, was found dead after apparently leaping out the window of a high rise. Her death foreshadowed Calvi's own, which came the very next day.

Calvi's corpse was discovered strung up by a rope, dangling under a bridge. But it wasn't just any bridge—it was the Blackfriars Bridge across the Thames River. Why is this significant? Because it would later be discovered that a secretive branch of Freemasons installed in the Vatican, known as the Propaganda Due (P2) lodge—or sometimes the *frati neri* (black friars!)—just might have been involved in Calvi's death.

Even without any inkling of a conspiratorial cabal, though, most who saw Calvi's corpse felt that he had met with foul play. Suicide was well within the realm of possibility, of course. Calvi had already tried it during his brief stint in prison, and with his mounting legal and financial problems he certainly had plenty of reason to consider ending his life. Nevertheless, his death seemed highly staged—if it *was* a suicide, Calvi certainly had a flair for the melodramatic—and there were several obvious red flags.

The first was the simple fact that the place he was found hanging, directly over the Thames, would have been nearly impossible for him to have gotten to without help. It was also strange that his pockets were stuffed with bricks, yet there were no fingerprints or any other evidence that Calvi had ever laid a finger on the bricks himself. It looked a lot like someone else had stuffed the bricks into his pockets, taken him to the middle of the bridge, and hanged him there.

There was thus quite a bit of skepticism when Scotland Yard ruled that Calvi had taken his own life, and his family, in particular, just weren't buying it. They hired investigators to look into whether one of Calvi's many enemies might have chosen to have him silenced. But these private eyes turned up nothing, and British police stuck with their official proclamation of suicide.

It wasn't until 2002, when Calvi's body was exhumed and a new autopsy was performed, that murder was once again deemed a possibility. Reopening the cold case in 2003, investigators soon found a brand-new treasure trove of information. They discovered that Italian Mafiosi had been laundering money through Banco Ambrosiano, sparking immediate speculation that Calvi's death was a Mafia hit performed both in reprisal for money lost and to silence the disgraced banker.

Another chilling detail that came out in this new inquest was that an associate of Calvi, Sergio Vaccari, who had helped arrange his escape to England, had himself been murdered a few months after Calvi was found dangling from Blackfriars Bridge. And if that's not enough of a coincidence to get you thinking, consider this: Vaccari was found with bricks in his pockets. Yes, you heard that right. The man who had helped Calvi flee was also found dead with bricks in his pockets. The bricks, an odd but innocuous side note before, now seemed like something else entirely—they seemed like the calling card of a killer.

But while the Mafia kills plenty of people, they don't leave bricks on their victims. So who does? Would you believe the Freemasons? After this detail was correlated with the fact that both the Vatican and the Mafia had ties with the P2 lodge, it was speculated that the bricks represented Freemasonry. And these P2 lodgers were also avid patrons of Calvi's banking operation before it all went south.

According to one former mobster, Francesco Di Carlo, Calvi's killing was a collaborative effort of P2 and the Mafia. In a 1991 interview, Francesco gave his reasoning as follows:

"Calvi was naming names. No one had any trust in him anymore. He owed a lot of money. His friends had all distanced themselves. Everyone wanted to get rid of him. He had been arrested and he had started to talk. Then he had tried to kill himself by cutting his wrists. He was released, but knew he could be rearrested at any time. He was weak, he was a broken man. I was not the one who hanged Calvi. One day I may write the full story, but the real killers will never be brought to justice because they are being protected by the Italian state, by members of the P2 masonic lodge. They have massive power. They are made up of a mixture of politicians, bank presidents, the military, top security and so on. This is a case that they continue to open and close again and again but it will never be resolved. The higher you go, the less evidence you will find."

Based on Di Carlo's testimony, Mafiosi Giuseppe Calo, Flavio Carboni, Manuela Kleinszig, Ernesto Diotallevi and Silvano Vittor were all put on trial for Roberto Calvi's death in 2005. However, there was no solid evidence against them, and the charges did not stick.

At around the same time, another shady figure, Licio Gelli, the supposed former grand master of the P2 masonic lodge, also came out of the woodwork. Gelli turned attention back to the Catholic Church, as he vociferously proclaimed that the hit was sanctioned by none other than the papacy. His reasoning can be boiled down to just one thing—motive. Because according to Gelli, if anyone had reason to get rid of Roberto Calvi it would have been the Vatican, since the Catholic Church had so many shady dealings with him. Gelli gave the strong impression that if all the information on the subject were allowed to come out, the Vatican would be rocked by a scandal of such proportions that even the Swiss Guard would have been unable to protect the papacy from its repercussions.

Well, maybe. But whether the order came from the papacy or not, the Vatican would indeed seem to have benefited from Calvi's abrupt silencing. Was this only a convenient coincidence? Roberto Calvi was the ultimate insider and perhaps the only one who could really answer that question. But of course, since his fatal trip to Blackfriars Bridge in 1982, he's not talking.

Alois Estermann and the Swiss Swirl of Conspiracy

It was one of the most notorious events to occur on Vatican soil. Some two decades after the 1978 demise of Pope John Paul I, members of the Swiss Guard sworn to protect the pontiff were involved in an alleged murder–suicide on May 4, 1998.

At the center of this drama was a young guardsman—just 23 years of age—by the name of Cédric Tornay. As the official narrative goes, Tornay, who was upset with the Commander of the Guard, Alois Estermann, suddenly snapped and killed Estermann, along with his wife Gladys, in a fit of rage before turning his weapon on himself. Nearly a year later, the official ruling stated, "the Estermann couple was killed by Vice-Corporal Tornay, who then immediately took his own life with the same regulation pistol."

But almost immediately a collective cry of "Not so fast!" echoed around Vatican City. And the loudest of those voices belonged to Tornay's mother, Muguette Baudat. Now, no mother would want to believe that her son had committed such a heinous crime, but Muguette had some especially solid reasons for her objection to the official narrative, and they centered on the note that her son had supposedly left for her before he shot the Estermanns and himself. Just by glancing at the message, she knew that Cédric could not have written it—because it wasn't in his handwriting! And the contents made it even clearer to her that whoever wrote the note, it was not her son. Here it is in its entirety:

Vatican 4-05-98

Mama,
I hope you will forgive me, for it is they who made me to do what I have done. This year I should have received the Benemereni but the Lieutenant-Colonel refused to give it to me. After 3 years, 6 months and 6 days spent here putting up with all kinds of injustice, he refused to give me the only thing I

wanted. I owe this duty to the remaining guards as well as to the Catholic Church. I took an oath to give my life for the Pope and that is what I am doing. Forgive me for leaving you all alone but my duty calls me. Tell Sarah, Melinda, and Papa that I love you all.
A big kiss to the greatest Mother in the World.
Your son who loves you.

The "Benemereni" mentioned in this missive is a medal that Swiss Guards typically receive after a few years of service. And it was no secret that Vice-Corporal Tornay had had a falling out with Lieutenant-Colonel Estermann and had been temporarily blocked from receiving his Benemereni. He was eventually given the medal, however, so it seems odd that he would still be angry enough to kill Estermann over that snub.

There were other irregularities in the note as well. First of all, the dateline, *Vatican 4-05-98*, was in a format that Tornay had never used before. Muguette knew that her son always wrote the date by writing out the name of the month first, followed by the day as an ordinal number, followed by the full year. So instead of writing *4-05-98*, Cédric would have written the date as *May 4th, 1998*.

That may seem like a minor, possibly insignificant detail, but as the letter continued, the inconsistencies only grew. It referred to Estermann, who had recently been made a full colonel, as "Lieutenant-Colonel", a mistake Tornay was not likely to make. And it referred to Tornay's sister as "Melinda" when he himself normally called her by her nickname of "Dada." Muguette asserts that even under the stress of writing his suicide note, her son would have used "Dada" instead of "Melinda". Furthermore, the note failed to mention Tornay's step-siblings at all, even though they were just as important to him as his biological sisters were.

And then there was the fact that the penmanship looked nothing like Tornay's handwriting.

Muguette has long alleged that her son didn't write the letter and that it was instead forged by someone who was familiar with the Vatican's personnel file on him. The file would have mentioned that Tornay had a sister named Melinda, but it would not have disclosed that he called her "Dada". Nor would it have revealed the close bond Tornay had with his step-siblings. To Muguette, it's clear that the "suicide note" is actually a forgery created to cover up something else. As she emphatically stated to the press, "The three people killed were the victims of a plot, and the official version is full of deceit, contradictions and lies in order to hide a probably inadmissible truth."

Muguette's theory is that Colonel Estermann must have "seen or known something" that the establishment didn't wish to be disclosed and thus needed to be eliminated. As for Estermann's wife and her son? They were apparently just collateral damage. Estermann was gunned down by a professional hit squad, and Gladys and Tornay were just in the wrong place at the wrong time. But for the killers, this proved to be very convenient. Seizing on Tornay's old grudge against Estermann, they happily took the opportunity to make it look like he had been the perpetrator.

But if all that is true, one would have to ask, why was Estermann targeted in the first place? Well, one conspiracy theory alleges that Estermann was not the man that others thought he was: he was actually an agent for the Stasi (the East German secret police) assigned to keep an eye on the Polish pope, John Paul II. Obviously, the pope's efforts in Poland—in particular, the Catholic Church's secret funding of the anti-communist Solidarity movement—would have been of great interest to the neighboring communist state. Another allegation is that the

Estermanns—Alois and Gladys both—were using secret channels at the Vatican to wheel and deal for the infamous Catholic secret society known as Opus Dei.

In an apparent attempt to counter these conspiracy theories, the Vatican released autopsy reports stating that Tornay had had a brain tumor the size of a pigeon egg and had tested positive for cannabis. The insinuation was clear: somehow, by virtue of being a pothead and having a brain tumor, Tornay had become mentally unhinged enough to commit murder. But there was a slight problem with this version of events as well, because right up until his death Tornay had been a highly esteemed and trusted member of the Swiss Guard. In fact, he had just been promoted to Vice-Corporal. If he was a mentally ill drug addict, wouldn't he have been drummed out of the Guard instead?

Another strange—and as it turns out, false—assertion in the autopsy report was that Tornay's body was in absolutely horrible shape. Muguette was initially told that her son's head had been nearly "ripped off" by the gun blast. She believed that this disinformation was intended to dissuade her from coming to her son's funeral. As she later recalled, "From the start I was the victim of pressures, manipulation, dissimulation and lies."

Things got even worse for the grieving mother when Cardinal Sodano himself met with her in regard to her many inquiries into her son's death. According to Muguette, "[Sodano] wanted to find out how much I knew and what I planned to do about it. He gave me a rosary, but he also threatened me in the name of his superiors, telling me I should stop asking about Tornay's death and think of my surviving children. He said he was sure I wouldn't want anything bad happen to them. That's a threat isn't it?" Well, it sure sounds like one—in many ways the language is reminiscent of a Mafioso perpetrating a shakedown. There is no explicit threat of injury, but the fact that Sodano mentioned the possibility of "something bad happening" seems to allude to it.

Muguette, meanwhile, had a bombshell of her own to drop. Little did Vatican officials know it, but shortly before her son died he had revealed to her that he and some of his fellow guardsmen were in the midst of an investigation into the dealings of the ultra-secretive Catholic group known as Opus Dei. That was about all he'd said—except to chillingly inform his mother, "The less you know about it, the better." And this may have been accurate, because as any conspiracy theorist will tell you, those wishing to keep the secrets of Opus Dei... well, secret are quite willing to kill to do it.

Adding another wrinkle to this mystery, it turns out that both Estermanns were very close to the shadowy organization. This was later confirmed by a Vatican intelligence operative named Yvon Bertorello who had been attempting to assess just how much Opus Dei had infiltrated the Swiss Guard. Bertorello had met Tornay shortly before his demise and recruited him into the investigation. Some have speculated that Estermann got wind of this and decided to confront Tornay, leading to a gun battle in which both men, as well as Gladys, were killed.

It has further been revealed that Estermann's promotion had been delayed out of concern over his close ties with Opus Dei. It was feared that he would essentially serve as a spy for the group, conveying invaluable details about the Vatican, the cardinals, and the pope's daily life.

Sadly, for the still grieving mother of Cédric Tornay, there are still no easy answers as to what happened to her son. This mysterious drama is one that continues to be played out.

Guarding the World's Largest Closet

We live in a world that is rife with whistleblowers and informants calling out corrupt organizations left and right. The Swiss Guard is most certainly no exception, and the most recent member to come forward with his own story to tell was nothing short of a former Commander of the Guard. Elmar Mader served from 2002 to 2008, and during that period he bore witness to a few things that he would never forget.

The biggest eye opener, he says, was the hypocrisy of priests who routinely condemn all things LGBT and yet are secretly gay themselves. According to Mader, this is an incredibly common phenomenon—and an organized one. He claims that during his time with the Swiss Guard he uncovered an elaborate homosexual network within the Vatican with the dual purpose of satisfying the needs of homosexual priests while simultaneously covering up their tracks.

Furthermore, as Mader tells it, it wasn't just priests. Many a young Swiss Guardsman found himself swept up in this seedy underground world as well. Once Mader realized what was going on, he felt it was his duty to warn the younger guardsmen that they might be preyed upon by some of the priests. Under his leadership, victimized guards finally felt emboldened to speak up, and several of them ended up reporting unwanted sexual advances. One guard even claimed that he was the victim of over *twenty* unwanted "unambiguous sexual requests". The alleged instances of sexual harassment range from chilling to absurd. One guard recalled how, as dinner was being served, a priest leered at him and proclaimed, "And you are the dessert." It might be tempting to laugh such things off, but harassment is harassment all the same. These young men were sworn to protect the pope, but they hadn't signed up to fend off the flirting and coercion of lecherous old homosexual priests.

And as shocking as these accusations are, they're actually part and parcel with the other scandals that have rocked the Vatican in recent years. Mader himself is no apologist for the improper conduct of priests, but he does understand that the culture and history of Rome and the Catholic Church have helped to create the climate that exists. According to him, it all really began with the very beginning of the priesthood. To be sure, some dedicated priests sworn to celibacy are serious about avoiding physical intimacy of all kinds. But as Mader points out, in the past, when gay lifestyles were completely forbidden and entirely hidden, the Church essentially served as a large closet into which to stuff gay men. Within the walls of the Vatican, their aversion to having sexual relations with women wouldn't be frowned upon—in fact, it would be celebrated. It was actually just about the only place where they could be accepted within the context of the society they lived in. Under the shield of the Church, a life that would otherwise have been deemed odd was made into a respectable vocation.

According to Mader, "a working environment in which the great majority of men are unmarried is per se a draw for homosexuals, whether they consciously seek it out or unconsciously follow an urge. The Roman curia is exactly this kind of environment." Mader stresses that he doesn't "have a problem with homosexuality" or even "gay priests" in the Vatican. His problem, he contends, is with this vast network that has been built up under the radar as a top-secret entity, and as such, is creating another layer of conspiracy and intrigue in an institution already rife with it. Mader is of the opinion that forcing priests into a status where they must express their urges in secret can only lead to problems and scandal in the long run. He is also worried about the issues of loyalty and security, noting that in his experience, the members of the gay network were more "inclined to be loyal to each other than to other people or institutions." Mader then goes on to proclaim, "If this loyalty were to go as far as to become a network or even a kind of secret society, I would not tolerate it in my sphere of decision making. Key people in the Vatican now seem to think similarly."

Mader is not without his own critics, of course. Some have condemned him for being homophobic and spreading fear and lies in regard to both homosexuality and the Vatican. And some simply believe that he is just way too paranoid for his own good. As for fears of a gay takeover of the Vatican, as Gaynet chairman Franco Grillini put it in one of his arguments against Mader's theorizing, "Statistically, gays are the least violent group in human society, so if the pope were really surrounded by homosexuals, he could sleep easy."

For now, though, the closeted doors of the Vatican just might hide the most closely guarded open secret the world has ever known.

The Bliss of Being Swiss

The Swiss Guard has a long history of service to the papacy—over 500 years, to be exact. During this time, the guardsmen have proven themselves to be extraordinary heroes who go above and beyond their call of duty during times of crisis. This was dramatically demonstrated at the dawn of their history when a couple hundred Swiss Guards fended off Europe's most massive army just long enough to allow their pope to escape to the safety of his fortress. This incredible valor was also evident in 1981 during the attempted assassination of Pope John Paul II.

So the Swiss Guards have a much-deserved reputation for being duty-bound warriors, but in recent years, conspiracy and intrigue have outshined their courageous past. It just goes to show you that in any ancient institution, there are bound to be cracks at the seams eventually.

In light of some of the more recent difficulties within the Guard, such as the shocking murder of Alois Estermann in 1998, it is actually quite reassuring that in 500 years' time, we haven't heard of even worst instances of fratricide and internal conflict. Looking at the history of the Guard in its entirety takes the edge off some of the more shocking highlights, and in general, being a member of the Guard, bearing a halberd, and standing sentry in brightly colored pantaloons appears to be quite a blissful profession.

Further Readings

As we bring this book to a close, let's take the time to go over some of the reading and reference materials that helped to make it all possible. Here you will find resources that continue the discussion of many of the topics touched upon here. Feel free to browse through them on your own.

The Swiss Guard Massacre: The Vatican Mysteries Vol. 1. Jacopo Pezzan & Giacomo Brunoro
These is a fairly recent book that revisits the killing of Alois Estermann and his wife Gladys in 1998. Although it does not have quite all the facts that you might expect for a case as wide ranging as this one. The basic core of the narrative is there. If you are interested in the incident, this book is a good place to start.

Murder in the Vatican: The Revolutionary Life of John Paul, the CIA, Opus Dei, and the 1978 Murders. Lucien Gregoire
This book focusses on the untimely demise of John Paul I and all of the many conspiracy theories that surround it. The book weaves such a twisted web of conspiracy it is sometimes hard to follow; but other than that, it's a good read.

The Annals of Unsolved Crime. Edward Jay Epstein
This book has a lot of good wide-ranging information on many unsolved crimes throughout history and as it pertains to this book, it takes a look at the attempted assassination of John Paul II. It is of course, interesting to note that on the official level the crime of the attempted hit on John Paul II's life is said to be solved in the form of Adci's arrest, yet of course many around

the world just don't buy it; including the author of this book. Here in this treatise, Epstein takes us down the road of conspiracy and back again.

Operation Gladio: The Unholy Alliance between The Vatican, The CIA, and The Mafia. Paul L. Williams
This book is complex to say the least. Just as the name implies, it follows thread after thread of intrigue between The Vatican, The CIA and the Mafia. Some of the mentions here need to be taken with a grain of salt but there are many eye-opening passages in this text all the same.

www.mysteriousuniverse.com
Mysterious universe is a repository of all things strange and mysterious and quite a few of the tales presented in this book are covered on the mysterious universe site. From the Vatican Banking scandal to the Swiss Guard scandal—there is certainly plenty to talk about when you pay this site a visit.

www.theguardian.com
The Guardian actually did a really good job of covering the Tornay incident. Here you can find reports going all the way back to 1998 when it occurred. Being able to read the facts from some of the original sources is tremendously helpful. If you are interested in this case, it's worth checking out.

Also by Conrad Bauer

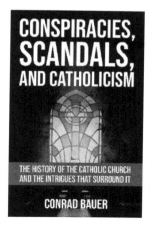 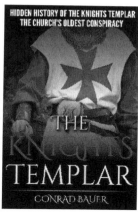 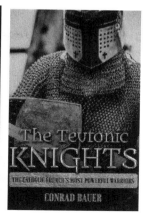

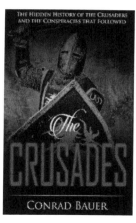 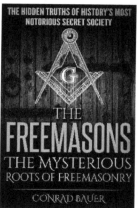 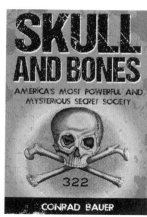

 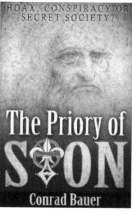 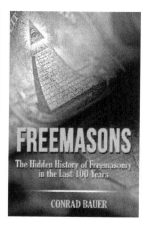

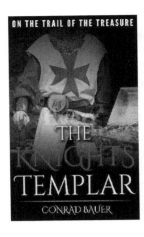  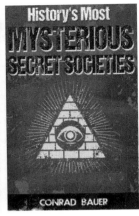

Image Credits

1. By Alexreavis - Own work, CC BY-SA 3.0,
   https://commons.wikimedia.org/w/index.php?curid=29111144

2. By José Cruz/Abr - Agência Brasil [1], CC BY 3.0 br,
   https://commons.wikimedia.org/w/index.php?curid=115911

3. Public domain,
   https://commons.wikimedia.org/w/index.php?curid=4888186

4. By Arnaud Gaillard, CC BY-SA 1.0,
   https://commons.wikimedia.org/w/index.php?curid=94194

5. By Vincent de Groot, CC BY-SA 4.0,
   https://commons.wikimedia.org/w/index.php?curid=467766

Made in the USA
Las Vegas, NV
15 February 2024

85729900R00026